Three Heavens And You

by

Roberts Liardon

Unless otherwise indicated, all Scripture quotations are taken from the *King James Version* of the Bible.

Some quotations are taken from the *New King James Version* of the Bible. Copyright © 1979, 1980, 1982, by Thomas Nelson Inc., publishers.

1st Printing

Three Heavens And You
ISBN 1-890900-13-3

Copyright © 1999 by Roberts Liardon Ministries
P.O. Box 30710
Laguna Hills, CA 92654

Published by Embassy Publishing Co.
P.O. Box 3500
Laguna Hills, California 92654

Contents

Contents

Introduction

I knew a man in Christ above fourteen years ago, (whether in the body, I cannot tell; or whether out of the body, I cannot tell: God knoweth;) such an one caught up to the third heaven.

2 Cor 12:2

Notice in this verse that Paul says he was: *"caught up to the third heaven."* If there's a third heaven, there has to be a second heaven, and if there's a second heaven, there has to be a first. It's amazing how many folks don't know that there's a second heaven, let alone a third. But according to the Bible, we have a relationship with all three.

I wrote this book to help you understand how to relate to each of the three heavens. As you will see, there are different garments that people are supposed to wear in each of the heavens. If you are not fully clothed in all three, you will experience a life of continual sin, heartbreak, disappointment and defeat.

5

1

The First Heaven

The first heaven is the earth's atmosphere, the climate of our planet. Everyone deals with the natural climates that exist throughout the earth.

When I lived in Oklahoma, summertime temperatures soared to 119 degrees. It was so hot that even the birds in the trees would pant! When I moved to Minnesota, it was a different climate altogether. Sometimes the temperature reached 14 below zero! The first time I went outside there and took a deep breath, my nose stuck together! Thank God He moved me to Southern California!

Proper Attire

In the first heaven we wear natural clothing. Everyone on earth has a relationship to the weather and they know how to dress accordingly. You don't go into an Oklahoma summer dressed like you're in a Minnesota winter. If you do, you'll die of heat stroke! Likewise, you can't go out in a Minnesota winter dressed like you're in an Oklahoma summer — you'll freeze to death in a matter of moments.

The Lord has a lot to say about what we wear for natural clothing. His Word says that He wants us to dress modestly. (1 Tim 2:9) I wish Californians would get a revelation of this because they wear as little as they can get away with in public. The Lord didn't tell us to run around in our underwear and call it our swim suit! Christians, of all people, should know better than that!

"But Brother Roberts, I want to do whatever I want on my own time."

Once you've been bought with a price, my friend, you have no time of your own! All your time belongs to God!

You have to dress appropriately as a Christian. It doesn't mean you can't be fashionable, it just means you should dress with modesty.

Don't Take Your Clothes Off!

A few years ago, a lady came into my church with hardly anything on. She didn't realize that it was wrong because she wasn't raised around the things of God. Some people dress with as little as they can get away with.

I was in a service one time when a guy started taking off his shirt. When an usher ran back there to stop him, the guy said, "The Lord told me to take my clothes off."

The fellow didn't look mentally disturbed at all, he looked normal; but it was obvious that he was affected by demonic powers. The Lord says, "Put your clothes on," and the devil always says, "take them off."

Abusing Your Body Effects Your Mind!

Devils want you to take your clothes off and do weird things to your body. What you do with your body effects your mind! Millions today have lost the ability to know right from wrong. They've lost modesty and they've forgotten what it is. You watch them walk down the beaches, down the streets, or through the malls. I sometimes think that someone should talk to them. It's no wonder that many 13 and 14-year-old-girls are already sexually active! God wants people to dress properly. That goes for the guys as well! We always accuse girls of dressing in ways that seduce men. Men can do the same thing too. We should all know how to dress properly. God wants us to dress nice and be good looking, but He doesn't want us to dress in a seductive way.

So we see that everybody on earth has learned how to dress and live according to the first heaven and that's good, but that's where most people's knowledge of the heavens stops. Most don't even know that the second heaven exists and they vaguely know about the third.

2

The Second Heaven

The second heaven is the world beyond your eyesight called, the spirit world. There are three different groups of beings that operate in the realm of the spirit. The first is God and His angelic armies, the second is Lucifer and all of his demonic hosts, and the third are human beings. Everyone on earth has some form of relationship with the second heaven. The second heaven is more dominant over human affairs than most people realize.

In Ephesians 6:10, we see that God gave us clothing to wear in the realm of the spirit. Our clothing in the second heaven is the armor of God.

Put on the whole armour of God, that ye may be able to stand against the wiles of the devil. For we wrestle not against flesh and blood, but against principalities, against powers, against the rulers of the darkness of this world, against spiritual wickedness in high places. Wherefore take unto you the whole armour of God, that ye may be able to withstand in the evil day, and having done all, to stand. Stand therefore, having your loins girt about with truth, and having on the breastplate of righteousness; And your feet shod with the preparation of the gospel of peace; Above all, taking the shield of faith, wherewith ye shall be able to quench all the fiery darts of the wicked. And take the helmet of salvation, and the sword of the Spirit, which is the word of God...

Eph 6:13-17

I praise God that He didn't leave us naked in the second heaven, because we need to be dressed there for sure. Notice that this scripture says, *"Put on..."* That is not a suggestion — that's a command. *"Put on the whole armor of God."*

God wants you to put *all* His armor on, not just part of it. There are a lot of Christians running around wearing helmets of salvation, but they're wearing nothing from the neck down. They forgot to put on their breastplate, belt, girdle and shoes.

If someone walked into your church with just a baseball cap on and nothing else, everybody would react drastically! But that's the way many today are dressed in the spirit.

The helmet of salvation is probably the most used piece of armor, but it's not the only piece. Every piece of the armor of God plays an important role in the life of the believer.

Many Christians just wear their helmet and their shoes — they got saved by an evangelist, and they attend an evangelistic church that's pastored by an evangelist. It's good that they have an evangelistic mentality, but they forgot about the rest of God's armor. They have their shoes and helmet on, but the rest of them is bare. That's why they're suffering with a bad spiritual self-image. They forgot to put on their breastplate of righteousness and the belt of truth.

Witchcraft Vs. Divine Spiritual Activity

With all of the spiritualism that is in the earth today, people have become more aware of the second heaven than ever before. That's why the Bible tells us to, *"Put on the whole armor of God, that ye may be able to withstand in the evil day…"* What is the evil day? It's the day when the devil is carrying out his wicked schemes.

We must become more aware of how strong the second heaven's influence over the earth is. In the spirit world there are demon powers that influence the affairs of the earth. But the Spirit of God moves there too. It's through Him that Christians find access to the second heaven.

The Church is the only group of people that has been given the right by God to teach people how to be spiritual. That's why He gave us the Holy Spirit! The only legal right into the second heaven is by the Holy Spirit's help and guidance. Any other entrance into the second heaven is an illegal entrance; it's witchcraft and spiritualism.

More than half of the books on angels that are in bookstores today contain the accounts of demons that people have met. They're not really angels from heaven, they're angels of light that come in disguise to bring deception.

Conditions In The Second Heaven

Out of all the types of clothing God could have given us to wear in the second heaven, He chose to give us armor. Why? Because of the hostile conditions that rage there. Armor indicates conflict and warfare; there is always a battle ensuing in the spirit world.

If you're entering into the second heaven without your armor on, you're going to get into trouble. You can't enter into a raging spiritual battle without God's armor and the Holy Spirit's protection. That's the reason many of God's people are in captivity and don't know how to get out. They're bleeding and dying because they don't have the right kind of clothing on.

In verse 11 we read, *"Put on the whole armor of God, that you may be able to stand against the wiles of the devil."*

So what's this armor for? It's for standing against the devil! It's not so you can march in a parade! When you get to Heaven, God is not going to reward you according to how shiny your armor is! He will reward you according to how tattered and dented it is!

The armor was given for war. If God didn't want you to be able to do battle in the spirit realm, He wouldn't have given you armor! He'd have given you some other kind of clothing. You won't need armor when you're in the third heaven! The devil is not there, disease is not there, temptation is not there. The armor of God is for the conflicts that take place in the second heaven.

Misinformed

I've heard some say that when you leave this world, you have to wait in the second heaven until the Lord comes back for you. They think that God gave us spiritual armor to protect us while we're there waiting. But that's totally unscriptural.

I can't understand why people who are so interested in spiritual things never take the time to read the most spiritual book ever written. The Bible tells us how to live in the spirit and how to operate in the realm of the spirit the right way, so it will be a blessing and not a curse.

Some people don't like to function in accordance with the Bible because selfish ambition, witchcraft and self-serving attitudes are not allowed.

The Holy Bible prescribes a supernaturally empowered life under the direction of the Holy Spirit. Under the Holy Spirit's direction you will do good things to humanity, and you'll be a blessing to people — even to them that are without faith in Jesus Christ.

Spiritualism is mainly for selfish gain and self-centered ambition. It has no rules or regulations. Occultists say they encounter spirits that once lived in Napoleon and Hitler. That's possible, but if I was going to reach out for something in the spirit world, I wouldn't reach out for a Hitler devil, or an Indian guru spirit who wants you to offer a piece of meat to a tree!

It's time to put on our armor and keep it on! Only then will we be able to prevail against the demonic powers that operate in the second heaven.

3

The Third Heaven

The third heaven is the world where the throne of God resides. It's where those who have died in Christ now live. It's the place where those who have been born again through faith in Jesus will live one day.

According to the Bible, the Heaven that we will go to at the time of the rapture will one day fade away and be replaced with a new Heaven. It will be a better Heaven than the one we know now. I don't know how the new Heaven could possibly be better than the old one, but I'm willing to go experience it.

The only way you can get to the third Heaven is by believing in Jesus Christ. You can't get there by humming a mantra or meditating with your legs crossed in front of a garden of flowers! You can only get to Heaven by a heartfelt confession of faith in the Lord Jesus Christ.

The Robe of Righteousness

I will greatly rejoice in the LORD, my soul shall be joyful in my God; for He has clothed me with the garments of salvation, he has covered me with the robe of righteousness, as a bridegroom decks himself with ornaments, and as a bride adorns herself with her jewels.

Isa 61:10 (**NKJ**)

There are special garments that God gives to everyone who lives in the third Heaven. Everyone there wears a white robe of righteousness. (Rev 3:5-6, Rev 3:18, Rev 7:9, Rev 7:13-17, Rev 7:14, Rev 19:14)

Around the throne were twenty-four thrones, and on the thrones I saw twenty-four elders sitting, clothed in white robes; and they had crowns of gold on their heads.

Rev 4:4 (**NKJ**)

Then a white robe was given to each of them; and it was said to them that they should rest a little while longer, until both the number of their fellow servants and their brethren, who would be killed as they were, was completed.

Rev 6:11 (**NKJ**)

One Family In Heaven and Earth

In the book of Ephesians we get another glimpse into the characteristics of the third heaven. The Apostle Paul writes:

For this reason I bow my knees to the Father of our Lord Jesus Christ, from whom the whole family in Heaven and earth is named...

Eph 3:14-15 (NKJ)

Notice that this passage didn't say there were two different families in two different locations. It said there was *one* family in Heaven and earth.

There is a close interaction between Christians and the third heaven — the place where the throne of God resides. Number one, our prayers ascend directly to His throne. When we pray on the earth, our prayers go right through the first heaven with no problem. But once in a while, our answer will have a problem getting back down through the second heaven. But if we pray with faith in the Name of Jesus, our prayers pass through the second heaven and go straight to His throne. That's one of the great mysteries of prayer; how prayer can be made at any time, anywhere on the earth, and immediately find it's place in the throne room of God, where the Father and the Son are listening.

The Center of Angelic Activity

The third heaven is where the angels of God ascend and descend from. It's the place that angels call home. Angels live and work out of heaven. So when they get done with the day's duty, when they want to go home, they go back to Heaven.

Some angels never go home. The one that's been assigned to you is stuck here for awhile. We would call that angel a guardian angel.

But to which of the angels has He ever said: "Sit at My right hand, till I make Your enemies Your footstool"? Are they not all ministering spirits sent forth to minister for those who will inherit salvation?

Heb 1:13-14 (NKJ)

So we have a prayer relationship with the third heaven. We have angelic workings that come from Heaven and we also have family members and friends that are there.

Our family and friends are aware, to some degree, of the movements of our life on the earth. I don't think they're aware of everything in full detail, but I do think they're aware to some degree. In much the same way, we are aware at times of what our family is doing in Heaven. Prayer is still being made for you there. Intercession is still being made by the saints that have gone on, and passed over to the other side. (Heb 7:25)

4

Put On Your Clothes!

Some Christians today are more concerned about natural fashion than what they are wearing in the spirit world. It's time to put on the right clothes! Wearing the right clothes gives you the ability to be joyful while you're here on the earth. It's no wonder people want to bail out! They're always getting hit with fiery darts and their feet are bloody because they're not wearing their gospel shoes! They have no shields so they wear themselves out trying to dodge the fiery darts of the enemy! No wonder they're miserable and they have no fun in their life!

Put your clothes on, my brother and sister! Come to the house of God and get dressed!

A Word of Prophecy

"For there are those of you who suffer many things, says the Spirit of God, and you have cried out to Me, yes

*some in recent times, you have cried out asking Me to
deliver you from that which you're going through. For
many of you have said, 'God, deliver me!'*

And the Word of the Lord comes unto me saying, "I
have delivered you by providing you with the right type of
spiritual armor so you can go through what you're in
without being affected by it. For some people pray for
deliverance, but they're not supposed to be removed from
that situation. They are to know how to live rightly in it,
and bring success, and bring victory right where I've placed
them. For many do run to and fro, but not by My sending,
but by their own fear, and by their own hardship. For My
end-time people must know how to remain where I've put
them. They need to know how to stay where I've told them
to stay, and how to labor where I've placed them.*

*"For I have provided for you with clothing that will
cause you to live victoriously, clothing that will give you
joy, clothing that will give you protection in the midst of
great hostile environments. So don't run to and fro, learn
how to remain where I've placed you. For the to and fro is
of the wicked one, he drives one here and drives another
there. But I have placed you, and equipped you to abide,
and equipped you to build, and equipped you to stay in
victory there, until My leading does come to show you the
next place you are to go.*

*"For many that are running, are not running by My
direction, says the Lord. They're running out of fear, out*

of pain, and out of agony because they have not prepared themselves to stay where I have put them. They have not dressed accordingly.

"So this day, as I have said to you, put on the armor and wear it well. Don't take it off, for it is your protection until your home-going, says the Spirit of the Lord.

"For there are also some of you that suffer continually in one area, says the Spirit of the Lord. There are some of you that suffer over, and over in areas of your life, and the problem never seems to fade away. There are torments that have been there since your childhood and have not left you. And you ask Me daily 'Oh Lord when will you deliver me from these things; when will you cause the enemy to go?'

"And the word of the Lord comes unto me saying again, 'It's because one part of your armor is not fully being worn. You're missing a part of your armor. Go back and investigate those consistent torments, and find out what piece of armor you've let fall to your side and pick it back up and tie it tight. Let it not fall again. Then you'll find the freedom and deliverance that you wish to have, says the Spirit of the Lord.

"For some have been tempted to live like other men, and they have not kept their eyes upon their example, Jesus Christ. They have done what other men have done and wore their armor for awhile. But then when they had grown tired of wearing it, they took it off, and some have never

put it back on. They've lost the armor that I have given them.

"*Let you who hear this, obey. Run quickly and put your armor on, for the days ahead will be demanding. They will demand much more work, labor, and conflict than what you have known in your past. So prepare now and know that the armor that I've given you is the only way you'll find protection and safety, for you have been divinely equipped to face every life struggle and every spiritual torment. In every place I send My troops, My armor will bring success and victory, quickly and easily.*

"*But them that try to obey without being fully dressed are always caught and put into captivity. Many are deceived and become as the earth would say, 'brain-washed' into thinking other things. That is why My end-time army must be fully clothed and prepared.*

"*The fiery darts of the enemy shall come in greater multiples than they have in years past. For the enemy does see and understand time better than My people, says the Spirit of the Lord. He wishes to wage a stronger battle, and a stronger war than in the years before.*

"*But if you are fully dressed and have been fully prepared, oh you shall have great joy in conquering and winning over the evil one.*

"*Be ready, for the new millennium will hold greater battles and greater conflicts. If you are dressed, it will not seem as such, but for them that are not dressed, they'll say how tough it is. You'll even see some fall away, and run back to their old lifestyles and run back to their old spirituality. And some will even say, It was I that led them to go back. They will think that they are out of My will.*

"*Know this, you've heard it before it occurs says the Spirit of the Lord. They'll run because they're not dressed. They'll run because they're not prepared. They'll run back to the old and say that the Lord told them to go back. So let every one of God's people be prepared and quickly grab their clothes and put them where they belong. Tighten them, and let them not fall off and let them not fall from their sides.*

"*Those whose hearts are not fixed will be the first to be lost. The hearts who have not fixed themselves upon the purpose and the pursuit of those things that I've placed before them, shall be quickly deceived and they shall fade away. Those fiery darts will come quickly to deceive.*

"*As you are dressing, make sure that your heart is fixed upon the divine calls that I have given to each of you corporately, and those things I have given each of you individually. For those who's hearts are not fixed, will be easily deceived and they will quickly fall away. There are even those now who have begun to take side steps from the righteous path. They don't see it as a wrong step. They don't know that it is a direction that will lead to destruction.*

"*So let those who have ears to hear today, heed the Word of the Lord. Guard your heart! Check in with your heart! Make sure that it is fixed! There are those even now who have already begun to go down the road of destruction! This day the Spirit of God and His mercy comes to bring warning; to bring alertness! The fiery darts are coming to bring destruction!*

"*The enemy will lie quietly. He will bring a false sense of security, making many believe that they're in the will of the Father. Then at the right time, great sorrows will come! There will be a great crying out! 'Why? Why?'*

"*Know this, I have told you now what to do so you can avoid many of these things in your life, says the Spirit of the Lord.*

"**Much preparation still has to be done, much educating still has to take place.** *Much more training of the natural man still has to come, so that My greater power, when it comes, can remain productive in the earth. I don't want it to be lost, as it has in the past.*

"*For there are false words that have been said by men that call themselves prophetic. Even over many of you, some of them have spoken. They have spoken of change. Heed not those words, says the Spirit of God, for My preparation, the season of My dealings, the season of My education and preparing is still upon you. Do not try to change seasons until I, says the Spirit of the Lord, decide for them to be changed.*

Put On Your Clothes!

"For if you change early, you'll find yourself wanting. For if you do, you'll find yourself entangled with the affairs of this life, assuming that they were the affairs of My leading. But they were not! Hear ye the Word of the Lord, and be quick to obey, for some do sit on the verge of great decisions that will cause them lifetimes of heartache and inward sorrow, says the Spirit of the Lord.

"For My seasons do not change according to the flow of man's emotion. For man's emotion goes up, and it goes down. My seasons do not change like that, nor do My seasons understand when men ask, how long? My seasons have no understanding of long and short!

"Many are saying how long must I remain doing this? Until God says it's done, until God says you've finished that course in your life! When men change courses and seasons, the whole plan that I have for them is sometimes aborted. Yes, they do good works in the earth, but it's not My high plan! Thus, the fruit that they do produce, not all of it remains as I had planned.

"And many of you, even you young ones, think how long I must stay doing these deeds, and doing these works, or walking this way? Oh, the Spirit of grace does say, until the Father decrees that it's done! Not before, and not after!

"So don't be in a hurry, for your hurriedness does cause you to miss things! Your hurriedness causes you to miss impartations, to miss revelations, to miss lessons that God has planned for you to learn!

"Don't rush, don't rush, don't rush! Stay in the season that God has placed you! Idle words and idle talk make men move in wrong directions! Idle words, unnecessary conversations, unnecessary discussions that need not to be discussed! For it's not even time for these things to be considered! You're missing divine time! That's why some of your hearts are discontented, that's why some of you are not happy as you once were! You've allowed yourself to become loose, in your words and conversation, says the Spirit of God. You've caused other men and women who are outside of My perfect will, to come and attack you! It's because you've moved outside of My will and timing for your life.

"Run back, says the Spirit of God. Run back into My will and say no more! Run back and discuss no more, run back quick and talk no more to them that have gone another way! They have gone out of My perfect plan, out of My perfect work for their life. Run back, says the Spirit of God, run back! Run, run, run! Run quickly before there comes an addiction to that kind of life. Run fast before there comes the wrong attraction to that kind of life!

"It's not a life of sin and evil, but it's a life of little compromises here and there. Things over which you say, 'Oh, that's okay, it's not that big of a deal.' It's those things that I'm warning you about today. It's not the gross sins and the romantic rebellions that are the most hurtful — it is these small ones.

"And this day I come to you warning that these things must change, or there will come dramatic happenings that will not be from Me, says the Spirit of the Lord."

A Prayer For You

If that word was for you, respond to it quickly. Lift your hands toward Heaven and begin calling out to the Lord.

"Father, we put on the whole armor of God! We take inventory of our heart and we make sure it's fixed. We also take notice of our conversations and distractions. Holy Spirit, come over these dear readers, and help the light to shine where there is darkness, cloudiness, and deception. We want to be prepared for what is ahead of us. We want to stay in the season of God, until You change it."

In Jesus' Name, Amen.

Notes

Notes

Notes

BOOKS
by Roberts Liardon

A Call To Action

Cry Of The Spirit

Extremists, Radicals and Non-Conformists

Final Approach

Forget Not His Benefits

God's Generals

Haunted Houses, Ghosts, And Demons

Holding To The Word of The Lord

I Saw Heaven

Kathryn Kuhlman

Knowing People By The Spirit

On Her Knees

Religious Politics

Run To The Battle

School of The Spirit

Sharpening Your Discernment

Smith Wigglesworth - Complete Collection

Smith Wigglesworth Speaks To Students

Spiritual Timing

The Invading Force

The Most Dangerous Place To Be

The Price of Spiritual Power

The Quest For Spiritual Hunger

Three Outs and You're In

To place an order call (949) 833-3555
or visit our website at: www.robertsliardon.org

AUDIO TAPES *by Roberts Liardon*

Acts of The Holy Spirit

Be Strong In The Lord

Breaking the Cycle of Failure

Changing Spiritual Climates

God's Secret Agents

Haunted Houses, Ghosts, & Demons

How To Combat Demonic Forces

How To Stay On The Mountaintop

How To Stir Up Your Calling
and Walk In Your Gifts

How To Survive An Attack

Increasing Your Spiritual Capacity

I Saw Heaven

Life & Ministry of Kathryn Kuhlman

Living On The Offensive

No More Religion

Obtaining Your Financial Harvest

Occupy 'Til He Comes

Personality of the Holy Spirit

Prayer 1 - How I Learned To Pray

Prayer 2 - Lost In The Spirit

Reformers & Revivalists

Rivers of Living Water (Grams)

School of The Spirit

Seven Steps of Demonic Posession

Sharpening Your Discernment (One)

Sharpening Your Discernment (Two)

Spirit Life

Spiritual Climates

Storms of His Presence

Taking A City

Tired? How To Live In The
Divine Life of God

True Spiritual Strength

The Anointing

The Healing Evangelists

The Charges of St. Paul - 1 Timothy

The Charges of St. Paul - 2 Timothy

The Working of Miracles
& Divine Health

Three Arenas of Authority
& Conflict

Three Worlds: God, You,
& The Devil

Tired? How To Live In The
Divine Life Of God

Tongues And Their Diversities

True Spiritual Strength

Useable Faith

Victorious Living In The Last Days

Working The Word

What You Need To Keep
Under To Go Over

Your Faith Stops The Devil

*To place an order call (949) 833-3555
or visit our website at: www.robertsliardon.org*

Spirit Life Partner

Roberts Liardon

Wouldn't It Be Great...

- If you could send 500 missionaries to the nations of the earth?
- If you could travel 250,000 air miles, boldly preaching the Word of God in 93 nations?
- If you could strengthen and train the next generation of God's leaders?
- If you could translate 23 books and distribute them into 37 countries?

...Now You Can!

Maybe you can't go, but by supporting this ministry every month, your gift can help to communicate the gospel around the world.

Roberts Liardon Ministries is sending Gospel missionaries to the hard and remote places of the earth!

------------------[CLIP ALONG LINE & MAIL TO ROBERTS LIARDON MINISTRIES.]------------------

☐ **YES!!** Pastor Roberts, I want to support your work in the kingdom of God by becoming a **SPIRIT LIFE PARTNER.** Please find enclosed my first monthly gift.

Name _____

Address _____

City _____ State _____ Zip _____

Phone (_____) _____

SPIRIT LIFE PARTNER AMOUNT: $ _____

☐ Check / Money Order   ☐ VISA   ☐ American Express   ☐ Discover   ☐ MasterCard

☐☐☐☐☐ ☐☐☐☐ ☐☐☐☐☐ ☐☐☐☐

Name On Card_____ Exp. Date___ / ___ / ___

Signature_____ Date ___ / ___ / ___

Roberts Liardon Ministries

P.O. Box 30710 ♦ Laguna Hills, CA 92654 ♦ (949) 833-3555 ♦ Fax (949) 833.9555 ♦ www.robertsliardon.org

IF YOU WANT TO
GO
THEN COME!

The nations are waiting for you!

Call Today!

(949) 833.3555

Seven reasons you should attend Spirit Life Bible College

1. SLBC is a **spiritual school** with an academic support; not an academic school with a spiritual touch.

2. SLBC teachers are **successful ministers** in their own right. Pastor Roberts Liardon will not allow failure to be imparted into his students.

3. SLBC is a member of **Oral Roberts University Educational Fellowship** and is **fully accredited** by the International Christian Accreditation Association.

4. SLBC hosts monthly seminars with some of the **world's greatest** ministers who add another element, anointing and impartation to the students' lives.

Send for your **FREE Video** of Spirit Life Bible College today!

5. Roberts Liardon understands your commitment to come to SLBC and commits himself to students by **ministering weekly** in classroom settings.

6. SLBC provides **hands-on** ministerial training.

7. SLBC provides ministry opportunity through its **post-graduate placement program**.

CLIP ALONG LINE & MAIL TO ROBERTS LIARDON MINISTRIES.

☐ **YES!** Pastor Roberts, please rush me a **FREE VIDEO** and information packet for **SPIRIT LIFE BIBLE COLLEGE**.

Name_____

Address_____

City_____ State _____ Zip _____

Phone (   )_____

Roberts Liardon Ministries
P.O. Box 30710 ♦ Laguna Hills, CA 92654-0710
(949) 833.3555 ♦ Fax (949) 833.9555
www.robertsliardon.org

VIDEO TAPES *by Roberts Liardon*

2+2=4

And The Cloud Came

A New Generation

Apostles, Prophets
   & Territorial Churches

Apostolic Alignment

Are You A Prophet?

Confronting The Brazen Heavens

Developing An Excellent Spirit

Don't Break Rank

Does Your Pastor Carry A Knife?

Forget Not His Benefits

God's Explosive Weapons

How To Be An End Time Servant

How To Be Healed
   of Spiritual Blindness

I Saw Heaven

Ministering To The Lord

No More Walls

Reformers And Revivalists (5 Vol.)

Spirit of Evangelism

The Importance of Praying
   In Tongues

The Lord Is A Warrior

The Most Dangerous Place To Be

The New Millennium Roar

The Operation of Exhortation

The Word of The Lord Came
   Unto Me Saying

True And False Manifestations

Was Jesus Religious?

Why God Wrote Verse 28

New God's Generals Video Collection

Volume 1 - John Alexander Dowie

Volume 2 - Maria Woodworth-Etter

Volume 3 - Evan Roberts

Volume 4 - Charles F. Parham &
             William J. Seymour

Volume 5 - John G. Lake

Volume 6 - Smith Wigglesworth

Volume 7 - Aimee Semple
             McPherson

Volume 8 - William Branham

Volume 9 - Jack Coe

Volume 10 - A. A. Allen

Volume 11 - Kathryn Kuhlman

Volume 12 - Highlights
             & Live Footage

Videos by Gladoylene Moore (Grams)

Foundations of Stone

God of the Breakthrough

How I Learned To Pray

How To Avoid Disaster

Seeking God

The Prophetic Flow

The Sword Of Gideon

The Warrior Names of God

*To place an order call (949) 833-3555
or visit our website at: www.robertsliardon.org*

ROBERTS LIARDON MINISTRIES
INTERNATIONAL OFFICES

EUROPE
Roberts Liardon Ministries
P.O. Box 295
Welwyn Garden City
AL7 2ZG
England
011-44-1707-327-222

SOUTH AFRICA
Roberts Liardon Ministries
P.O. Box 3155
Kimberely 8300
South Africa
011-27-53-832-1207

AUSTRALIA
Roberts Liardon Ministries
P.O. Box 7
Kingsgrove, NSW
1480
Australia
011-61-500-555-056

Roberts Liardon Ministries

P.O. Box 30710
Laguna Hills, California, USA
92654-0710
Telephone: (949) 833-3555
Fax: (949) 833-9555
Visit our website at: www.robertsliardon.org